ROBERT H BICKMEYER

---

# LAUGHTER IN REAL LIFE

---

and a few jokes

and a few words of wisdom

**Think Club Publications**
P.O. Box 451
Bloomfield Hills, MI 48303-0451, USA

Copyright © 2007 by Robert H. Bickmeyer

The author owns all rights to the essays and columns in this collection, but wishes to acknowledge the following magazines and newspapers in which some of the pieces previously appeared.

Dear Abby
The Detroit News
Detroit Free Press
Daily Tribune
Daughters of American Revolution Publication
Sons of American Revolution Publication
Metro Times
Military Magazine
Oakland Press
Olive Branch Press
The Think Club
Vintage Views
Washington Times
Chicken Soup for the Soul

Cover Photo Copyright © David Beagan

ISBN 978-0-9672833-3-3

Printed in the United States of America
January 2008

# Dedication

*For Phyllis, my Sunshine,
who has brought so much
sunshine into my life.*

**To the Readers of this Book**

These pages contain the humor seen, heard, spoken and remembered by the author as well as a few personal thoughts and observations.

At the end of each chapter is a blank page for you to add your humor, thoughts and observations.

# Contents

| | | |
|---|---|---:|
| Introduction | | 1 |
| 1 | A Few Family Funnies | 3 |
| 2 | Child Chuckles | 10 |
| 3 | The Terrible Teens | 20 |
| 4A | Adulthood - True Tales | 27 |
| 4B | Adulthood – Fiction (Jokes) | 44 |
| 4C | Adulthood An Interlude Of Seriousness | 52 |
| 5A | Senior Humor – True Tales | 61 |
| 5B | Senior Humor-Fiction (Jokes) | 81 |
| 6 | Wit At Work | 85 |
| 7 | Political Humor | 99 |
| 8 | Sidesplitting Sports Stuff | 104 |
| 9 | Vacation Heehaws | 117 |
| 10 | One-Liners | 122 |
| 11A | Military Humor – Fiction | 126 |
| 11B | Military Humor – True Tales And "The Sarge" | 129 |
| 12 | … And That's The Way It Was! | 138 |

# Introduction

I guess dear old Dad passed on to me the genes that gave him a love for laughing or to make others laugh. Dad was always ready with a funny remark or, with garden hoses in hand, quick to spray the lady next door. At least he thought it was funny. I'm not sure Mrs. McCarthy though so. He would go to extreme lengths to get laughs.

Dad's best effort was the time he went to great pains to pretend he was his own sister. Mother and a group of friends met once a week to play Bridge. When they met at a nearby neighbor's house one time, Dad rang the front doorbell, wearing lipstick, a wig and Mother's dress. Using a falsetto voice he introduced himself as his own sister. He had the group of women confused and wondering, "Is this absurd woman really John's sister?" Until, one-by-one, they realized it was John himself and, one-by-one, laughed uncontrollably. Dad had fun. And I've been having fun all my life.

Thank you, Dad, for the fun genes and examples of fun you gave me.

Americans are now more health conscious than ever before. At most social gatherings the latest diet fad is discussed. Many are on exercise programs to burn calories, control blood pressure and maintain healthy functioning hearts and lungs.

The entire medical profession agrees that good humor is a tonic for good health. It is intended that, as you read, you will laugh or chuckle or grin inwardly to put you in a healthy frame of mind. This book will be a long-lasting health pill. Have fun.

Your children will enjoy this book. If you have no children your grandchildren will enjoy it.

# 1
# A Few Family Funnies

In the 1940s our small garage was a separate structure be hind our house. One cold night when Dad pulled into the driveway he thoughtfully stopped near the back door so Mom, my sister and I could exit the car and hurry into the house.

Hurry we did, as Sis and I left the car's two rear doors open. Dad then pulled into the narrow garage, stopping only when he heard a loud crunch behind each ear.

ಐ ಛ ಐ ಛ

Dad had a 1939 Plymouth during World War II and our dog, Blackie knew it was "his" car. It was only when our Plymouth was parked in front of our house, no other car, when Blackie would draw warm chuckles from our neighbors. What did he do? He'd step onto the running board, then up onto the fender, to the hood and finally onto the roof. There he would lay as if to say, "This is my car."

ಐ ಛ ಐ ಛ

Bobby was five when I brought home our first new car with power windows. We went for a family drive. Keep in mind, there were no seat belts to keep our children in their seats back then. I soon heard a scream behind me. Turning around I saw Bobby's head sticking out of the window, caught between the glass and the top of the window frame. Playing with the new toy, he had opened the window, struck his head out and, with the mentality of a five-year-old, closed the window.

I immediately opened the window and, luckily, only his pride was hurt.

My mother, who had often been irritated by the fact that I tend to drive fast, had a fender bender when a young man drove through a full stop sign. A few months later she had another minor accident due to the carelessness of another driver who rammed into her. While visiting her and talking about her two misfortunes now twelve-year-old Bobby asked, "Dad, why don't you ever have any accidents?" Before I could reply, Mother said, "Because he drives so darn fast no one can catch him to hit him."

Prior to my wife's scheduled open-heart by-pass surgery I attended a lecture given by the hospital to prepare family members for the lengthy recuperation. About a dozen of us were told, among other things, "They will feel like they had been hit by a truck. They will be in the hospital about seven days afterward; it will take six to eight weeks for full recovery. Any questions?"

I asked, "How long will it be before my wife can do my laundry?"

ಸಂ ಆ ಸಂ ಆ

On answering my telephone I heard my daughter say, "Hi Dad, are you busy?"

When I said, "No, I was just at my typewriter typing a letter."

Linda cracked, "You dinosaur," to which I replied, "Not so, it's an electric typewriter."

ಸಂ ಆ ಸಂ ಆ

Those blunt methods of letting guests know it is time to go home are rude. My Uncle Charlie had a subtle, but unique way. During conversation he yawned. Since yawning is contagious, his company started yawning and, thinking they were tired went home to bed.

ಸಂ ಆ ಸಂ ಆ

My daughter and son-in-law were visiting from out-of-state and borrowed my car to go to the mall. On exiting the mall they realized they had not noted what my car looked like, not even the color. It was somewhere in the sea of cars before them. Car keys in hand, John realized my car was equipped with the keyless entry system. He simply walked up and down the lanes pressing the open trunk symbol until the trunk lid of my car popped open.

༄ ༅ ༄ ༅

Mom, Dad, sister Claire and I were sitting on our front stoop after supper one balmy summer evening. Plop, went some bird poop as it landed on one of the steps, luckily missing all of us. We laughed, but laughed even harder when Dad quickly said, "It's a good thing cows don't fly."

༄ ༅ ༄ ༅

My Jack Russell Terrier, Barkley, and I were taking our daily walk when a truck rumbled by. I tightened my grip on his leash, knowing he hates trucks, trying to chase and attack them. The truck driver pulled over to the curb a few houses past us to make a telephone call. As we reached the truck Barkley pulled the leash taut, trying to attack the truck. Knowing the parked truck could not hurt him, I allowed him to reach it. As he did, he clamped his teeth on the back edge of the front fender. The driver, looking down, laughingly said into his phone, "A dog is biting my truck."

ಸಂ ಶಿ ಸಂ ಶಿ

When my father, a veteran of World War I, was a young man his grandfather lived with Dad's family. Grandpa was a crotchety, complaining old man who was never happy. One day the old geezer said to my dad, "If I had a gun I'd shoot myself."

Dad said to him, "Here's a rope – hang yourself."

ಸಂ ಶಿ ಸಂ ಶಿ

My daughter, Linda, wore a new dress to church one Sunday. During the service Linda walked up to the alter to receive communion and back to her pew in the rear of the church. Later, while exiting church, a friend commented on the unique monogram on her dress, a vertical series of the letter "L." Looking down, Linda saw the clear strip of plastic with a series of Ls indicating her dress was size large.

Every family has funny incidents worth remembering and recording or incidents that are a lesson learned. Record them here for your descendants

# 2

# Child Chuckles

My wife, Phyllis, and I were taking a walk, our ten-month-old grandson in my arms. An elderly, dignified lady stopped us, saying to Phyllis, "Isn't he cute? He is absolutely adorable! How old is he?"

Before Phyllis could answer, I said, "I'll be 55 in July."

₪ ೦₰ ₪ ೦₰

Now that our "nest" is empty Phyllis and I easily control all noises in our home. She often speaks to me from kitchen while I'm in the next room watching television. I usually press the mute button on the remote control to silence the TV, the better to hear her. One day, while babysitting our infant granddaughter, Roxann, Phyllis spoke to me when the baby was crying. Without thinking, I pressed the mute button to silence her.

ಸಂ ಡಿ ಸಂ ಡಿ

Our daughter's home is one where the television is always on. Roxann, now two years old, was spending the day with us. After watching some morning talk shows I turned the TV off.

Looking up from her coloring book, Roxann asked, "Where are we going?"

ಸಂ ಡಿ ಸಂ ಡಿ

On another day I realized Roxann was no longer in the same room with me and called, "Roxann, where are you?"

Walking out of the bedroom with her head shaking back and forth, she said, "I not touching Grandma's lipstick."

ഒ ഇ ഒ ഇ

We were taking four-year-old Roxann up north to the Thumb area of Michigan to spend an eagerly awaited week in a cabin on Lake Huron, a 100-mile drive from our home in Troy. We had driven about three miles and, in fact, were still in Troy when Roxann's voice from the back seat was heard, "are we almost there?"

ഒ ഇ ഒ ഇ

We had just arrived at our rented cottage on the beach. Roxann walked out of the door with all of the toys from her sandbox at home. With the sandy beach only yards away, she called to Phyllis, "Grandma, where's the sandbox?"

ഒ ഇ ഒ ഇ

Phyllis was explaining something to Roxann, now five. Roxann, not understanding, said, "Wait grandma, rewind."

ഒ ഇ ഒ ഇ

As the waitress served Phyllis her hamburger and french fries I reached over and took one fry. Phyllis said, "If you take one more I'll shoot you."

Four-year-old Lindsay, after patiently waiting about two minutes, inquired, "Grandpa, when are you going to take one?"

༄ ༅ ༄ ༅

Casey, my three-year-old granddaughter, was sitting on my lap as I read her a story. Casey looked up to me lovingly (I thought), and said, "Grandpa, I see your boogers."

༄ ༅ ༄ ༅

After dinner, daughter Linda served ice cream for dessert. Casey, now four, couldn't finish hers so I pulled her dish in front of me.

Linda cautioned me, "Dad, I wouldn't eat that after her."

I said, "why not? She's my granddaughter."

Little Casey added, "Yeah, we have the same split, right Grandpa?"

༄ ༅ ༄ ༅

A few days later, as they drove me to the airport to head for home, I said, "I guess it will be good to have the old guy out of your house so everyone can get back to normal."

It was Casey again who said, "No, we like having the old guy around."

ಶಿ ಛ ಶಿ ಛ

My sister, Claire, expecting her third child, was explaining the miracle of birth to her little daughter Robin. "Our new baby is in my tummy, where you came from."

"Well, where did you come from, Mommy," asked Robin?

"I came from Grandma's tummy," replied my sister.

Said Robin, "How did you fit?"

ಶಿ ಛ ಶಿ ಛ

When my kindergarten-age son refused to eat the spoonful of spinach on his dish I remembered that Popeye was in his Saturday morning cartoon lineup.

I coaxed, "Who always eats spinach to make him strong?"

Bobby answered, "Not me!"

                                                    ✽ ✽ ✽ ✽

After studying about Abraham Lincoln our fourth grade class was instructed to write a composition about him. One classmate wrote: "Lincoln loved to read as a boy. He walked many miles to the library to borrow books. One Saturday he decided to go to the movies instead of the library where he was shot."

                                                    ✽ ✽ ✽ ✽

Douglas was in kindergarten where, I guess; he learned a new word – the "F" word. He knew it was a naughty word because he was obviously trying to shock me with it. He used it while we were watching television, he sitting on my lap. Rather than showing the shock he was looking for, I feigned interest in the TV and pretended not to hear him. He used it again. Still no response from Grandpa.

Determined, Douglas said, "Grandpa" as he took my chin in his hand and turned my head to face him. Looking me in the eye he said one word, the "F" word.

                                                    ✽ ✽ ✽ ✽

Joke:

Six-year-old Brian said to his five-year-old friend, Bobby, "Guess what? I found a condom on the veranda." Bobby asked, "What's a veranda?"

ೲ ೃ ೲ ೃ

My neighbors, with six-year-old Brandon, were visiting Grandpa in Florida. Arriving at the pool one morning, they found a group of senior ladies being led in an organized exercise class. They waited for the class to end.

When the ladies started to exit the pool Brandon asked one of them, "Why do you exercise?"

She replied, "To lose weight and be slim."

Looking her up and down little Brandon said seriously, "It's not working."

ೲ ೃ ೲ ೃ

My son took his seven-year-old son, Kenny, sleigh riding. Little daredevil Ken took much delight from speeding down the hill and steering over a large bump that sent his sled airborne. Since his landings were not always smooth he arrived home with scratches and bruises on his face.

The next day a visitor asked, "Ken, what happened to your face?"

Ken replied, straight-faced, "My Dad took me into an alley and beat me."

ಲ ಣ ಲ ಣ

An avid bicycle rider, I picked up a used pink, girl's bicycle at a garage sale to go for a ride with any of my grandchildren while visiting us.

The first time I tried to put it to use, my nine-year-old grandson, Bradley, rebelled with, "But that's a girl's bike and it's pink."

After using all the psychology and persuasiveness I could muster, Bradley reluctantly agreed to join me in a ride. A few blocks from home we came upon a garage sale. I turned into the driveway, Bradley behind me.

Looking at the lady-in-charge, he quickly explained, "This isn't my bike."

ಲ ಣ ಲ ಣ

My mother-in-law was, of course, our granddaughter's great grandma. The family reacted with a chuckle every time little Roxann, still learning to talk and unaware of any mispronounced word, called her "Grape grandma."

❧ ☙ ❧ ☙

While searching for my favorite cereal in the super market a young mother, with two small daughters, stood behind me.

I heard her whisper, "Who made a stinker?"

One little girl quickly said, "Not me," followed by the other, saying, "Not me".

The woman's perplexed look turned to one of disdain when I turned, looked over my shoulder and said, "Not me."

❧ ☙ ❧ ☙

Their mother was taking her two tots to spend a couple of days with their father before Christmas. The youngest cried, fearing he would not be home for Christmas when Santa was coming.

Seven-year-old Halle said to R. J., her five-year-old brother, "Christmas is three nights from now. We're staying with Daddy for two nights. Do the math."

What have your children or grandchildren said that you repeat to others for a laugh? Jot their bright sayings down here.

# 3

# The Terrible Teens

I, an immature teenager, had walked into my high school English class with a bottle of "skunk" perfume in my pocket. Before our English teacher arrived I uncapped the bottle, allowing the odor of rotten eggs to permeate the classroom. As the teacher strolled into the room I called to her, "What is that stink in here?"

"I don't know, "She replied, "but it wasn't here before you arrived."

ಸಿ ೧೩ ಸಿ ೧೩

On completing school I "fell" into a job in the officers of General Motors. I was still there 25 years later when my wife asked our son what kind of work he wanted to do. Bobby could not tell her.

Looking at me, she said, "Can you imagine, he's 15 and he doesn't know what he wants to be?"

I answered, "I'm 45 and I don't know what I want to be."

ಸಿ ೧೩ ಸಿ ೧೩

I had become tired of the touch-tone telephone system that slowly, step-by-step directs you to push numbers until you eventually complete your call.

One day I answered my ringing telephone with "Hello, if you would like to speak with Bob, press one. If you would like to speak with Phyllis, press two. "I heard a beep and asked, "What number did you press?"

John, my seventeen-year-old nephew's voice said, "Uh, two, is Aunt Phyllis there?"

My new car had the feature whereby the headlights automatically go out about ten seconds after the ignition is turned off.

One evening, as I walked away from my car, a youngster in a Boy Scout uniform called to me, "Sir, you forgot to turn off your lights."

Turning, I said, "Thank you, son."

Then I pointed at the car and said with emphasis, "Eenie meenie minee mow ... hocus pocus ... Kalamazoo" – and the lights went out. I again thanked the boy, as he stood there with a look of disbelief, before I walked away.

I had watched with pride as my grandson, Bradley, played a whale of a game for his high school football team.

A few nights later, as he left my house, he hugged me, saying, "Bye Grandpa."

I kissed him on his cheek. Looking at my wife, I said, "That's the first time I ever kissed a fullback."

Joke:

Three young brothers were talking about inventions. Kris, the eldest, cited the airplane as the very best invention ever.

"After all," he said, it defies gravity."

The second brother, Stephen, said, "I think the wheel is the best. Almost everything that moves, even the airplane, needs wheels."

Kenny, the youngest, added, "The best invention ever is the thermos. It keeps drinks cold in the summer and hot in the winter. How does it know?"

୫୦ ଔ ୫୦ ଔ

My eighth grade English teacher was a stern disciplinarian. Looking back, I realize she was a good teacher. Back then, I thought she was too tough and needed some diversion from her steady, intense teaching. I had the immature, devious mind of a 13-year-old, my age then. As she wrote on the blackboard I made some spitballs and, with my thumb, flicked them onto the ceiling all over the classroom.

"We'll change classes soon," I reasoned, "and my spitballs will dry during her next class, dropping all over the room and disrupting the class."

When the bell rang to change classes I took one more glance at the ceiling and left the room chuckling with delight. When I arrived at English class the next day there were my spitballs, all still stuck on the ceiling.

ಬಿ ಅ ಬಿ ಅ

Joke:

St. Peter dispatched an angel to earth to investigate the behavior of today's teenagers. On returning to Heaven the angle advised that his survey disclosed that only ten percent of teenagers make their bed in the morning and keep their rooms clean.

"What shall we do about that, St. Peter?" asked the angel.

"I don't know. We better have a meeting to decide what to do about the 90 percent who do not. Meanwhile, have plaques made to send to the ten percent."

As I told this story to my grandson I asked him, "Do you know what the plaques said?"

When he replied, "No, I don't," I said, "Didn't you get one?"

ꙮ ꙮ ꙮ ꙮ

There were four push buttons on my car radio. One was tuned to an all news station, one to a sports station, and one to an "oldies" music station. The fourth was pre-set to music my two teenage children, Linda and Bobby enjoyed, but I did not. One day, Bobby, sitting alongside of me, was listening to his station. Listening to the singer I decided for once, to enjoy his music – good parental psychology?

I said, "That I enjoy. She's a good singer."

Rolling his eyes, Bob said, "It's not a woman, it's a man."

The older you get the more likely you are to look back at teenage pranks by yourself or others with a chuckle or maybe disdain. Describe it here.

# 4A
# Adulthood –True Tales

D r. Milton Eisenhower, president of Johns Hopkins Hospital, was about to speak at a function in Pittsburgh. After being introduced as the president of "John Hopkins" he responded that it was a pleasure to speak in "Pittburgh."

ಬ ೧೪ ಬ ೧೪

A friend, recently returned to Michigan from New York City, was amazed by the similarities of many New Yorkers.

He once asked a New Yorker for the time of day and was met with the response, "Why doncha buy a watch?"

Before telling me how his question was answered, he asked me, "You're a former New Yorker, what would you say if I asked you for the time?"

He was astounded when I, unknowingly, blurted, "I'd ask you why you didn't buy a watch."

ಐ ಲ ಐ ಲ

It is my custom to test my vocabulary each month with the "It Pays To Enrich Your Word Power" test in the *Reader's Digest*. I habitually passed on my completed "Digest" to a good friend. One month, while testing my vocabulary, I realized my habit of checking my correct answers were exposing my knowledge (or lack of it) to my friend … so I put a check mark alongside all twenty answers.

ಐ ಲ ಐ ಲ

It happened in 1965 when New York State had implemented the policy of giving eye tests before a driver's license is renewed. I arrived at the Motor Vehicle Bureau before it opened. Instead of the expected wall chart I was asked to look into an electric viewer.

I looked into it, then looked at the clerk, saying, "It's not warmed up yet. All the letters are fuzzy."

She chuckled, "Sorry sir, you need glasses."

ଛ ଓଃ ଛ ଓଃ

The breakfast menu in a local family restaurant included toast with eggs. An English muffin could be ordered for an additional ten cents.

On giving my order for scrambled eggs I asked the waitress, "Do I understand the menu correctly, can I have an English muffin for ten cents?"

"That's right," she confirmed.

I said, "I'll take twelve."

ଛ ଓଃ ଛ ଓଃ

I have Christmas lights that are alive and actually move about between Christmases. Every January I neatly wrap them before storing them in the basement, but when I bring them up the following December they are always very tangled.

๛ ෬ ๛ ෬

A friend suspected that his wife was looking through his wallet at any opportunity. One evening he announced he was going into the shower. A few minutes after he entered the bathroom he turned on the shower and closed the shower door with a bit of a slam ... but he had not entered the shower stall. He waited about ten seconds, then quickly walked from the bathroom into the bedroom. His wife standing at his dresser looking at him – eyes wide, mouth open and his open wallet in her hands.

๛ ෬ ๛ ෬

We were two couples, applying for fishing licenses the morning of our one-day fishing expedition. Our description, including our weight, had to be shown on the license.

When the clerk asked my friend's wife her weight, she replied, with a smirk on her face, "119 pounds."

It was my wife's turn. In response to the same question and with a slightly wider smirk, she said, "118 pounds."

ഗ ര ഗ ര

I called a friend in Florida to wish him a happy birthday. He was not home so I sang "Happy Birthday" to him on his answering machine. He called later to thank me, adding, "Do me a favor next year, send me a card – don't sing!"

ഗ ര ഗ ര

As is the norm, I advised my wife we were late.

She reached a new height with her latest excuse, "You didn't hurry me up."

ഗ ര ഗ ര

I had just ordered roses in my local florist, to be delivered to my wife on Valentine's Day.

In response to my request for morning delivery the clerk explained, "I'm sorry, they are too busy on Valentine's Day to accommodate requests for specific time of day."

I suggested, "To be fair, then, deliveries should be made in alphabetical order."

ಸಿ ಅ ಸಿ ಅ

Stopped at a red light during the evening rush hour I was driving the third car in the right turn lane. The driver of the second car honked his horn to get the attention of the woman driving the first car, then motioned her to make a right turn, normally permitted on a red light. Getting out of her car, she walked to the curb and pointed to a sign reading "No right turn, permitted on red." then man in a hurry exited his car, ran to the curb and pointed to the smaller print immediately under "No right turn permitted on red" that read "Between 7 - 9 a.m."

ಸಿ ಅ ಸಿ ಅ

We were having a board of directors' meeting at our boys club in Whitestone, New York. Our treasurer reported that the new safe, previously authorized by the board, had arrived.

He lamented, "I don't know how to get rid of the old safe. The Sanitation Department advised me they can't take it because it exceeds their weight limit. Any ideas?"

After a few moments of silent thinking a board member suggested, "why don't we put it in front of our building at curbside in the morning and leave it there?"

We did. The following morning it was gone.

ഈ ⌘ ഈ ⌘

I often wonder which grave a local man wishes to be buried in or if he has instructed his undertaker to flip a coin. To the left of my wife's parents' graves is the grave of Mr. Smith's (not his real name) first wife. The headstone bears her name, the years of her birth and death and his name, but only his birth year. To the right of my in-law's graves is the grave of Smith's second wife. Her headstone, too, shows her year of birth and death and Smith's full name, again only his birth year. He has made provisions for his burial with both wives. Flip a coin?

ഈ ⌘ ഈ ⌘

A friend had a heated debate with his wife about a rule in the card game Bridge. He found the correct explanation in a book covering the game of Bridge and, gleefully showed her that "according to Hoyle" he was.

His wife sneered, "That's an old book."

Hearing this story, another friend said, "My wife is Miss Right ... and her first name is Always."

೫ ೧੪ ೫ ೧੪

Remember Y2K? Due to our reliance on computers, many feared that at the stroke of midnight, when the year 2000 arrived, power would fail, records would be lost and, heavens to Betsy, might the screens on our TVs go blank? My son, Bob, was at the home of his in-laws for a New Year's Eve party. A few minutes before midnight he slipped into the basement and located the circuit breaker. Listening to the countdown upstairs, at the stroke of midnight he plunged the house into darkness.

೫ ೧੪ ೫ ೧੪

It was a routine drive home from work during rush hour. All traffic, both directions, was at a standstill because a mother duck and her eight ducklings were waddling across the road. They moved very slowly while all normally impatient commuters were immobilized.

I grinned, watching the procession of ducks, then looked around, expecting to see a sea of glaring drivers. Surprisingly, without exception, everyone else was grinning too. My grin became a chuckle as I surveyed the scene. Momma duck and her brood and the tired but now happy workers were a scene I will always remember.

༄ ༅ ༄ ༅

A co-worker was paying his respects to the widow of a long-time friend. As he stood there talking to her, with his friend in a casket a few feet away, there was a lull in their conversation.

In order to break the awkward moment he asked, "So, what's new?"

༄ ༅ ༄ ༅

I was among many local extras in Detroit, hired for the filming of a courtroom scene in the movie "Hoffa." In the opening of the scene, Jimmy Hoffa (portrayed by Jack Nicholson) walks down the aisle toward the front of the courtroom.

A union man sitting in an aisle seat says, "Nice suit, Jimmy."

Hoffa stops, faces the man and says, "You like it? My wife picked it out just for today."

Director Danny DeVito ordered many takes so that we heard "Nice suit, Jimmy" many times. When we broke for lunch the extra who portrayed the union man sitting in the aisle seat happened to be in front of me on the buffet line. We were all dressed in 1950s style suits supplied by wardrobe.

I said to him, "Nice suit, Jimmy."

He grinned, saying, "Coincidentally, my name is Jimmy."

At another break later in the day the same union man strolled up to the urinal next to where I was.

I repeated, "Nice suit, Jimmy." He chuckled.

At the end of the day all extras returned to the wardrobe changing area, a large room where all men removed their 1950s suits to change into their own clothes. As I strolled in, there in front of me was Jimmy the union man, standing in his underwear.

He laughed heartily when I called out, "Nice suit, Jimmy."

෪ ෬ ෪ ෬

One winter lunch hour about six of us were gathered for conversation in the lobby of our office building. One man noted that a pretty young woman had been standing opposite the bank of elevators, apparently waiting for her lunch partner.

He said, "I'll bet a dime she's waiting for a handsome young guy."

Another added, "I'll bet she's waiting for a man old enough to be her father."

Another, "She's just waiting for another girl," until all made a guess except me.

I said, "I'll bet she's waiting for me."

I then walked across the lobby to her and explained our bet, saying, "Do me a little favor? Look at my group and point at me to indicate I'm the one you're waiting for."

She grinned, "I'll do better than that," and offering her arm, said, "Here, take my arm and we'll walk past them."

I did, but at that moment an elevator door opened and out stepped a tall, husky young man who glared at us. She said, "Oops, here's the one I'm really waiting for," and dropped me like a hot potato.

୨୦ ෬ ୨୦ ෬

My wife of Hungarian descent, Phyllis, and I were celebrating our wedding anniversary at a Hungarian restaurant in Detroit. The entertainment offered was an organist, a gypsy fortune teller and two strolling violinists with a guitar player. When our waiter learned it was our anniversary he asked our name.

Later in the evening, as the violinists approached our table, the organist announced to all the dinner guests, gesturing toward our table, "Today is Mr. Bickmeyer's anniversary." This was a little embarrassing to Mrs. Bickmeyer sitting with me, but not my fault she was overlooked.

He then asked, "Mr. Bickmeyer, do you have a request for our violinist?"

Admittedly, music appreciation is not one of my long suits. Having enjoyed one of the tunes they played earlier, I simply asked them to play it again, as I hummed the first few bars. Unfortunately, something was added to this performance – the guitarist sang the lyrics, unknown to me. Everyone in the restaurant listened and laughed as he sang:

> To all the girls I've loved before
>
> Who travelled in and out my door
>
> I'm glad they came along
>
> I dedicate this song
>
> To all the girls I've loved before.

This was very embarrassing to Phyllis and totally my fault, due to my ignorance of the song.

ಬ ಚಿ ಬ ಚಿ

A friend of my wife was having a cup of coffee with us at our kitchen table. On the table in front of me was our kitchen timer that I had set to remind me to do something. This timer does not sound off with a lone ring, but with a lengthy ring similar to that of a telephone. But it is obviously a timer, not a telephone.

When our kitchen talk was broken with the timer's lengthy ring I picked it up, held it to my ear and kiddingly said, "Hello?"

After a short pause I handed it to our friend, saying, "It's for you."

With a blank look on her face, as if wondering, "Who would call me here?" she took the timer, held it to her ear and said, "Hello?"

ನಿ ಲ ನಿ ಲ

It was almost blizzard-like weather when I walked into our local bakery early one Saturday morning.

As I waited my turn the man in front of me, selecting donuts, said, "Gee, I forget what kind she wanted."

The clerk asked, "She? Are they for your wife?"

The man's poker-face response was, "Of course, you don't think my mother would send me out in this weather do you?"

ನಿ ಲ ನಿ ಲ

Driving along I saw a sign on the side of the road, with sloppily painted letters, reading, "Painter needs work." Although the painter's telephone number was also on the sign it is my guess that he is still waiting for his first call.

ನಿ ಲ ನಿ ಲ

The newlyweds had a problem when they had to be somewhere at a given time. She was always late and he was always on time.

His weekly nagging and complaining failed to improve her punctuality.

Exasperated, she finally declared, "You should not enter a marriage expecting to change someone."

He agreed, "You're right ... so don't try to change me from someone who is always on time to someone who is always late."

80 03 80 03

Jack was a long time co-worker, also a friend. We bowled on the same team and golfed together. Known for his humor, at social gatherings everyone wanted to sit at the same table as Jack, thus guaranteeing a laughable, fun evening. He prized his annual trips to Las Vegas to do a little gambling. Two other enjoyments were a cold can of beer with a good cigar. He wasn't retired very long when God took him. As I viewed him in the funeral home I could almost detect a smile on his face. His sons' humor matched his. They had put a few cigars in his breast pocket, a can of beer was nestled in his arm and his hands had Las Vegas gambling chips placed in his fingers.

Phyllis, my wife and self-assigned "nurse," always insisted on accompanying me into any doctor's office to ensure I asked all the necessary questions and to hear his diagnosis and instructions. We were in my ophthalmologist's examining room during my siege of extreme sensitivity to light following cataract surgery.

I expressed my extreme dissatisfaction by telling him, "The biggest mistake I ever made was marrying my first wife. My second biggest mistake was agreeing to cataract surgery."

Phyllis, sitting in the corner, said, "I'm his second wife."

This space is for adult humor. Think about it – during your dating days or during marriage? – and write about it below for a permanent record.

# 4B Adulthood – Fiction (Jokes)

Suspecting my wife was suffering from a slight loss of hearing, I stood about 30 feet behind her and whispered her name. Hearing no response I moved to within 20 feet of her and again whispered her name. No response. After whispering from ten feet she answered, annoyingly, "For the third time, what do you want?"

A nun entered a convent where a vow of silence was mandated. After ten years the Mother Superior told her, "Every ten years you are permitted to say something. Is there something you would like to say?" The nun simply said, "The food could be better." At the end of the twentieth year she was again asked to speak. She said, "My room is cold." After thirty years the nun decided to leave the convent. Exasperated, the Mother Superior said, "I knew it, just what I expected. You've done nothing but complain ever since you arrived here."

Last week I took my wife to a very exclusive restaurant. While walking to our table I told her a joke. She laughed so hard she almost dropped her tray.

Joe, Vince and Jack were carpooling to a game of golf when a careless driver hit them head-on, an accident fatal to all three.

St. Peter met them at the Pearly Gates and, pointing out all the ducks in Heaven, cautioned them, "We love our ducks. Be careful not to step on one as the penalty is quite severe." Joe must not have listened too well as he quickly stepped on a duck. Two angels immediately chained him to an ugly old lady, telling him, "The penalty for stepping on one of our ducks is to be chained to this woman for eternity." Vince, thinking about the golf game he missed, soon stepped on a duck. He, too, was chained to an ugly old woman. Seeing this, Jack was very careful and never stepped on a duck. One day though, he was chained to Michelle Pfeiffer. Curious, Jack asked, "What happened?" Michelle answered, "I don't know. All I did was step on a duck."

෨ ෬ ෨ ෬

On October 19, 1879, after many failures, Thomas Edison finally succeeded in placing a filament of carbonized thread in a bulb. The bulb shed a good light. Although it was the wee hours of the next morning, he excitedly awakened his wife to share in his joy.

A sleepy Mrs. Edison said, "Tom, will you turn out the lights and come to bed?"

ಸಿ ಲ ಸಿ ಲ

While driving along a remote country road I came upon a one-legged hitchhiker. Seizing the opportunity to do a good deed I pulled over and told him, "Hop in."

ಸಿ ಲ ಸಿ ಲ

When in Rome, Colonel Sanders of Kentucky Fried Chicken obtained an audience with the Pope.

During their brief meeting he asked Pope John, "If you will change your prayer from 'give us this day our daily bread' to 'give us this day our daily chicken' I'll give you $500,000."

When the Pope declined his offer the colonel increased his offer to one million dollars. The Pope accepted.

The next day at a meeting with his Cardinals Pope John said, "I've got some good news and some bad news, I've acquired one million dollars that can be used to do much good in our church, but the bad news is, we've lost the Wonder Bread account."

ಸಿ ೧೮ ಸಿ ೧೮

At a dance my attention was drawn to a gaunt, elderly looking man who energetically danced every dance with variety of young women. When the band took a break I had my first opportunity to admiringly ask the gentleman what type of life he led that enabled him to maintain such a pace. He replied, "After working all day I spend a few hours drinking at my favorite bar before I come here to dance until he band goes home. Then I take a different girl home every night."

Amazed, I asked, "How old are you?"

"Twenty-eight" he beamed.

ಸಿ ೧೮ ಸಿ ೧೮

He had a habit of often stopping for a drink or two his way home from work. On one such stopover he had many drinks before he realized he had not called his wife. When he did, he stammered, "Hi Honey... er, uh ... listen ... uh ... what are you having for dinna t'night?"

His angry wife answered, "We're having horse manure."

He considerately said, "Well I won't be home for dinna so cook only half of it."

ಸಿ ಆ ಸಿ ಆ

A man's doctor called him one week after his examination. "I've got the results of your lab tests and … a … I've got bad news and worse news."

The man blurted, "Give me the bad news first."

"Well," said his doctor, "The tests show that you have only 24 hours to live."

"What?" cried the man, "What could be worse than that?"

His doctor advised, "I couldn't get in touch with you yesterday."

ಸಿ ಆ ಸಿ ಆ

After advising his doctor he had frequent dizziness, headaches and chills the man's doctor diagnosed, "I'm sorry, but you have only six months to live."

After a week of fretting the man decided to cheer himself up by buying a complete new outfit of clothes at a local men's clothing store. On selecting a size 15 shirt the store owner told him he was a size 16. The man insisted he was a 15.

"Sir," said the owner, "I've been in this business 30 years. If you wore a size 15 shirt you'd have dizziness, headaches and chills."

෴ ෴

Visiting his psychiatrist, the man described his mental problem, "Some days I think I'm a tepee, some days I think I'm a wigwam."

The psychiatrist's diagnosis was quick, "You're under too much stress, which makes you two tents."

෴ ෴

During an examination my doctor asked, "Have you been under any stress lately?"

I replied, "Yes, the past two hours while sitting in your waiting room."

**Know any good jokes? Keep them clean.**

# 4C

# Adulthood
# An Interlude Of Seriousness

The tide had receded, leaving thousands of starfish on the beach in the hot sun. A man saw another man pick up a starfish, walk to the water and throw it in. Walking back up the sandy beach he picked up another, walked back to the water and tossed it in.

The man watching asked, "There are thousands of them, what good can you do?"

Tossing another starfish into the water, he replied, "It did him some good."

ಐ ಛ ಐ ಛ

Like most seniors I believe everyone is entitled to my opinion, so I usually voice it. On moral issues such as homosexuality, abortion, out-of-wedlock births, unwed couples living together or obscenities I am sometimes told, "Hey, it's the 21st century, get with it."

My response, "The same God who judged us 100 years ago is judging us today" renders them speechless.

ಐ ಛ ಐ ಛ

We must often decide whether to do a chore first or to do a fun thing. Remember, dessert is always more delicious and satisfying after our vegetables have been eaten.

ಐ ಛ ಐ ಛ

Being short never really bothered me, but the insensitive barbs did.

I eventually learned that the response, "God made me short because He knew I could handle it," rendered them speechless.

When asked what my height is I sometimes said, "I'm six feet tall, but I'm short for my height."

☼ ☙ ☼ ☙

I think Tony Blair's, the former Prime Minister of Great Britain, assessment of the United States bears repeating.

"There is a simple way to take the true measure of a country – think about how many people want to get in and how many want to get out."

Pure gold!

☼ ☙ ☼ ☙

If you fear car theft, keep a note handy in your car to use when you park in an area with a high pilferage rate, like malls and airports. The note, reading "gas on empty" is left on the driver's seat as an apparent reminder to yourself, but hoping it will discourage a car thief who will not want to run out of gas with a stolen car.

I recommend you try it as car thieves will not read this book.

ଊ ଓ ଊ ଓ

One mother can take care of four children, but four children cannot take care of one mother. Too often, too true.

ଊ ଓ ଊ ଓ

Fact: keep in mind that 50 percent of all doctors graduated in the lower half of their class.

ଊ ଓ ଊ ଓ

One Christmas season I helped Santa Claus by filling in for him at a small shopping mall with few shoppers. Instead of the usual long line of children that are processed on and off Santa's lap like an assembly line, I was able to enjoy spontaneous visits of teenagers and adults as well as little tots bearing lists of toys.

A pair of 15-year-old boys ran up to me, hugged me lovingly and, grinning, each asked me to bring him a motorcycle. After a brief chat they walked away chuckling, pleased with their visit with St. Nick.

A very bright and happy 3½-year-old little girl sat on my lap and chatted constantly, asking questions and answering mine.

Finally, looking me in the eye, she said, "I thought you were fake. You're real!"

Her doubts removed, I am sure she had a magical Christmas.

A young father, all alone, paid the elf photographer for one picture and explained to me, "I don't have custody of my children and want to show them a picture of you and I shaking hands."

After receiving the finished photo and looking at it he mouthed "thank you" to me and departed.

My most emotional visit was the approach of three teenage girls. The first, giggling, asked me for a sports car. The second one topped her by asking for a mansion.

The last girl whispered in my ear, "I'd like a job for my father."

As they walked away the last one refused to answer her friends' probing questions, "What did you ask for?"

Her profound request was between her and Santa who was filled with unforgettable emotion.

I truly believe that the girl's father found a job because, you see, that night Santa prayed that he would.

☙ ❧ ☙ ❧

Do you really believe computers can predict the future? Let us assume we had computers 100 years ago. If all data available back then were fed to a computer it probably would have predicted that in 100 years all our highways would be covered with ten feet of horse manure.

☙ ❧ ☙ ❧

Do not put too much trust in kids. They have the mentality of a child.

☙ ❧ ☙ ❧

If I relate or read an interesting item to my wife, she is sometimes annoyed with the interruption of her own reading or TV watching. Similarly, if she reads something to me, I am sometimes annoyed. These minor annoyances, however, are preferable to not having someone to read to.

ಐ ೧೫ ಐ ೧೫

As we stashed our golf clubs in our car trunks, Jack and I complained bitterly about the atrocious golf game we both had. Reflecting about it, I said, partially joking but mostly seriously, "Jack, Jim and Tom are in nursing homes with Alzheimer's Disease and more than 20 of our close friends are in cemeteries. We're out here playing golf so we can't complain."

ಐ ೧೫ ಐ ೧೫

DREAMS – "he got up on the wrong side of the bed" is a cliché often used to describe someone who arises in the morning in an irritable or depressed state of mind.

I contend that these moods stem from a stressful or frightening dream they experienced shortly before awakening. Dreams are easily forgotten by our conscious mind, but their effects remain on our subconscious until the realities of the day take over. The duration of these effects will vary from a few seconds for some or up to a half hour or more for others.

Children are more likely to suffer from such dreams as they have more difficulty dealing with moods. Many of us, including myself, are plagued with them frequently.

If you are aware of why you "got up on the wrong side of the bed" (it was a bad dream) you will more easily overcome your bad mood and are more likely to "have a good day."

ಸಿ ಲ ಸಿ ಲ

If, in the beginning of a marriage or relationship, one partner is somewhat controlling or dictatorial the other might squelch such behavior by saying, "I will do almost anything you ask me to do … and nothing you tell me to do."

ಸಿ ಲ ಸಿ ಲ

The man who has no imagination has no wings.

– Muhammad Ali

A lesson learned from an adult experience might be recorded here for subsequent readers of this book.

# 5A

# Senior Humor – True Tales

My elderly mother was telling about her young neighbor on the sixth floor of her apartment building.

"She runs two miles in the park almost every day and she usually walks up and down the six flights of stairs when she comes and goes, instead of using the elevator. That girl is going to wear herself out and die young."

It was about 2 a.m. when the telephone rang. My friend's wife jumped out of bed to answer it. It was her mother-in-law, who asked, "Shirley, what are you doing up at this hour?"

Another friend made his weekly phone call to his mother in a nursing home in another state. During their talk she talked about her husband as if he was there beside her.

Bill patiently explained, "Mom, Dad can't be there with you. He died five years ago."

When he called her the following week she seemed more in touch with reality when she said, "I don't know what was wrong with me last week when I thought your dad was here with me."

Then she added, "He was sitting out in the TV room."

My mother, from New York where the city is surrounded with toll highways and its five boroughs are connected by many toll bridges, was visiting us in Michigan.

On a tour of the area we drove south through Detroit into Windsor, Canada where a customs agent leaned out of his booth, asking, "What country are you citizens of? Why are you coming here?"

After we answered his questions the agent smiled and told us to have a nice day as he waved us into Canada.

As we drove away Mother said, "That was the friendliest toll collector I have ever seen."

ಜ ಬ ಜ ಬ

Two of the men in our car pool lived across the street from one another. One retired. On the first day of his retirement we arrived at the usual time to pick up his neighbor. The retiree, in bathrobe and pajamas, was sitting at a table on his front lawn, reading a newspaper and sipping coffee. He greeted us with a wave and a smile. When we returned that evening he was sitting at the same table, nattily attired in sport clothes.

An even broader smile was on his face as he raised a cocktail towards us in toast-like fashion.

ಬಿ ಛಿ ಬಿ ಛಿ

After looking for my wife throughout our ranch style home – from the kitchen to the three bedrooms, in the bathroom, into the basement, I irritably called out, " Phyllis, where are you? "

From a corner of the family room came her voice, "In here, what do you want?"

Me: "I forget."

ಬಿ ಛಿ ಬಿ ಛಿ

Our over-55 softball team customarily goes to a local restaurant for lunch after our twice a week games. Maria, our pretty young waitress beams when we arrive, knowing she has a few chuckles coming. Gary, an Elvis impersonator, invariably walks in with his Elvis gear on and goes into his brief act for whatever customers are there.

Another teammate once said to Maria, "You get prettier every week ... and today you look like next week."

She had not stopped laughing when another senior said, "Hurry up with our orders. The bus from the nursing home is picking us up in an hour."

ഓ ൨ ഓ ൨

At one of our senior softball games one member of our team proudly introduced his two granddaughters to the team.

A teammate cautioned the girls, "Don't yell, 'Grandpa come here.' If you do, fifteen men will come running."

ഓ ൨ ഓ ൨

The headline "Caring for an aging parent" drew my attention to the article. As I began reading the advice I realized there was no need to as my mother-in-law had recently passed away, leaving Phyllis and I without parents.

As I related this to Phyllis, she said, "Send it to our children. We are now the aging parents."

ഓ ൨ ഓ ൨

Phyllis and I were both busy near the kitchen sink when I walked away.

She said, "Are you going to leave the water running?"

I replied, "I'm not the one who turned it on."

Embarrassed, Phyllis admitted, "Oh yeah, I did," as we laughed together at another "funny" in a home of the elderly.

ഔ ജ ഔ ജ

I am a five feet, five inch man in his mid seventies who exercises daily with a lengthy bicycle ride. I sometimes run errands during a ride so I mounted a basket on my handlebars.

When I mentioned this to my daughter, Linda said, "Dad, you're going to look like a little old man pedaling around town."

I replied, "Linda, I am a little old man."

ഔ ജ ഔ ജ

When my 65-year-old friend wanted to make use of the benefits of Viagra his doctor gave him a prescription for only ten pills to be sure they were effective for him.

He bragged to his doctor, "That's only a ten days supply."

His braggadocio was deflated when, arriving home, his wife asked him, "Why did the doctor give you a ten year supply?"

※ ※ ※ ※

While on a long line waiting for flu shots at our senior citizen center we arrived at a point where the line divides into two lines. Those on Medicare were directed to go right while the under-65 seniors were sent to the left. This parted the married couple in front of me.

The husband, with a sad look, said to his wife, "I'll meet you 20 years from today at the top of the Empire State Building."

※ ※ ※ ※

My mother-in-law's number one passion was shopping. My father-in-law kidded her so often about going "shoplifting," as he called it, that it became a substitute for the word "shopping" in his vocabulary. One evening after dining out they were threading themselves through a throng of diners waiting for tables. Mom said she didn't feel like going home.

Dad suggested aloud, "Well, let's go shoplifting."

I had occasion to call a former co-worker, now retired in Florida, who I had not spoken to in many years.

When he answered the phone I asked, "Is this Bob Gerhardt, formerly of College point, New York?"

He quickly said, "Yes, it is, Bob Bickmeyer."

Flattered that he knew it was me, I said, "Hey, you recognize my voice after all these years?"

He replied, "No, I have caller I.D."

After retiring at age 57 I became active in senior citizen softball, volleyball and golf.

Over the years I would occasionally say to some of my elderly teammates in their 70s, "Gee, I hope I'll still be playing when I'm your age."

Recently a 55-year-old rookie on our volleyball team said to me, "I hope I'll still be playing when I'm your age."

At a senior breakfast in Michigan we were discussing the pros and cons of the elderly shovelling snow.

One man bragged, "I like the exercise from shovelling it."

Another said he simply walked behind his self-propelled snowblower while another said he hired someone to remove his snow as even the cold air is bad for the heart.

I reminisced, "I, too, hire someone but when I was younger I shovelled my walks and when I wisely stopped to take a break I lit a cigarette."

ಐ ಙ ಐ ಙ

Our senior softball team was practicing for a game when 68-year-old Jim showed up after having surgery. We asked him how long before he'd be able to play ball.

He replied, "I intended to ask my doctor three questions: when can I mow the lawn, when can I make love and when can I play softball? The doctor told me to wait a week before I mowed the lawn, but I could love my wife that night.

I was so happy with that answer I forgot to ask about playing ball."

༺ ༻ ༺ ༻

While chatting on the phone with John, a friend and former co-worker who lives in Florida, I asked about another friend who lives near him.

When I asked if he still plays golf, John said, "Oh no, he's 84 now."

I replied, "I played golf today with Vince who is 84. In fact, he beat me."

༺ ༻ ༺ ༻

As we pulled out of a restaurant parking lot I noticed a young mother folding a stroller at the trunk of her car.

I remarked to my wife, who has congestive heart failure, "I'm glad we're beyond that stage of our lives. What a bother."

Phyllis replied, "Oh yeah, how about my folding wheel chair in our trunk?"

༺ ༻ ༺ ༻

As I backed our car out of the garage I hit the button in our new car to close the garage door. It did not close.

I hit the button repeatedly, but because of the frigid nine degree temperature, the door would not close. My wife, Phyllis, had to reach into the glove compartment for our old hand-held opener. It immediately closed the door.

As I backed out of the driveway I said, "Shucks, I forgot my glasses," frustrated because we then had to open the door so I could go back into the house for my glasses, then close the door again.

It was not necessary though because Phyllis said, "What's that on your face?"

෩ ෬ ෩ ෬

When visiting my daughter's family in New York we spend our nights in their comfortable, finished basement, with bed and bath. During one of their visits to us in Michigan I was astonished by the amount of food wasted by my two granddaughters.

When little Casey took one bite out of an apple and then dropped the apple into our kitchen trash can I said to my daughter, "Linda, if I ever have to live with you in my old age it won't cost you anything to feed me. Just give me the food the girls waste."

Linda grinned and said, "Yeah, I'll just open the basement door and toss it down to you."

ഌ ര ഌ ര

My audiologist was showcasing her assorted hearing aids. Holding one of them, she advised, "This one is designed for married men. It has an on-off switch."

ഌ ര ഌ ര

After a senior citizen softball game our team was, as usual, lunching at our favorite restaurant. When our friendly waitress teased one of the men he said, "You women are all alike. I have one at home." He then added, "There are two ways to handle women ... but I don't know either one of them."

ഌ ര ഌ ര

When my wife stopped by her mother's house for a brief visit Mom said, "How about a cup of coffee? I have a pot on the stove."

My coffee loving wife asked, "Is it fresh?"

Mom very seriously assured her, "Oh yes, I made it today."

ഌ ര ഌ ര

I lost a very close friend who was taken by a brain tumor. Bob's great sense of humor deepened the loss of those who loved him. When his doctor learned he had the tumor, the doctor tried to soften the bad news by telling Bob, "It could be serious malignancy or it may be a tumor you were born with and have carried all your life."

Bob straight-faced, "Oh, then that would explain why I had so much difficulty with long division."

※ ※ ※ ※

While standing in line behind a woman in a greeting card store I noticed she had selected a card that read "To My Best Friend." As I continued to look I saw that she was buying three of them.

※ ※ ※ ※

His grandson had recently bragged about his ability to read at a level above his own age. During grandpa's birthday celebration little Kenny asked grandpa how old he was. Gramps answered, "I'm 76, but I read at the level of a 77-year-old."

※ ※ ※ ※

At another post game lunch I ordered spinach quiche because I like spinach and it is healthy. A teammate teased me, "Real men don't each quiche."

I countered, "Real men eat anything they want!"

ಸಿ ಅಃ ಸಿ ಅಃ

During our annual visit to the Michigan State Fair my wife and I invariably paid the few dollars to have an "expert" guess our ages. Why? Because his guesses, for both of us were always much younger than our actual ages. Even though our prizes were never worth the few dollars we paid him, it was fun and most satisfying. A few years ago the expert guessed both of our ages within two years of our actual age. We stopped checking in with him. It wasn't fun anymore.

ಸಿ ಅಃ ಸಿ ಅಃ

A softball teammate arrived at practice wearing one blue sock and one red sock. When someone pointed out his wardrobe goof he replied, "It's a pair. In fact, I have another pair at home just like them."

ಸಿ ಅಃ ಸಿ ಅಃ

Our senior citizen volleyball team had decided to meet at a very busy, large restaurant for lunch after a league match. I had to make another stop en route to the restaurant and knew I would be the last to arrive. As I entered, a pretty young girl greeted me, offering to help me. I told her, "I'm looking for a bunch of old men."

My teammates reacted with assorted facial expressions when I told them this, adding, "She took me right to you guys."

ಸ ಐ ಸ ಐ

After our softball team's annual golf outing we had pizza and beer in the backyard of our leftfielder's home. As we sat at poolside re-hashing our season, making wisecracks and good conversation I noticed a teammate in his 70s, sitting hunched over, chin on his chest.

I asked the others, "Is Bill sleeping? With all this lively conservation?"

Doug answered, "Either he's sleeping or he died."

ಸ ಐ ಸ ಐ

Our softball games started at 10 a.m. during the season, but during the end-of-season playoffs at one multiple field complex where all games were played, the first games of the day began at 9 a.m. One teammate, Gary, complaining about this early start, wryly said, "Gee, we have to get up early, even before breakfast."

ಬ ಡಿ ಬ ಡಿ

I always keep a bottle of frozen water in my freezer to take with me on a hot day when I play golf or softball. Consequently, I constantly have ice water to sip on during my game. One softball teammate, a former school teacher, was embarrassed by my simple explanation when he asked, "Bob, how do you get the ice in the bottle?"

ಬ ಡಿ ಬ ಡಿ

It was our softball team's first game with our new uniforms. When an overweight teammate appeared wearing his obviously too small uniform T-shirt, another asked him, "What are you doing George, giving your shirt a stress test?"

ಬ ಡಿ ಬ ಡಿ

Jack and Will were the two best golfers in our large group. One day, when Will wasn't present, someone suggested we set up a match between the two of them. I quickly said, "I'll put my money on Will."

Jack, standing next to me, complained, "Thanks a lot, friend."

I grinned, "Well he cheats."

෨ ෬ ෨ ෬

Our senior citizen humor is continuous, especially with one teammate who never fails to ask for the senior discount. When the cashier looks at him he invariably points at his wrinkled face, asking, "Do you want to check my I.D.?"

෨ ෬ ෨ ෬

In one volleyball game two bald members of our team were dressed similarly and their height and builds were similar. This tended to confuse one member of the team who said, "During the action I don't know who is who. You're both wearing gray shorts, green shirts and have the same color hair."

෨ ෬ ෨ ෬

At a family restaurant, after an early volleyball match I ordered bacon and eggs. The waitress asked, "How would you like your eggs?"

I watched her face closely, seeing a perplexed look when I said without grinning, "One over easy, one scrambled."

**2001 SOFTBALL TEAM:**

**Seven in back row (L to R):**
Don Coomer, Dave Fabian, Angelo Bencivenga, Bob Okuska, Bill Dardy (Mgr.), Mike Marshall, Gary Mettie (Elvis).

**Six in front:**
Homer Welch, Nick Buccini, Bill Eckstein, Ed Forst, Dennis Guy, Bob Bickmeyer the laughing author.

We all know a few "funnies," but of the mouths of grandmas and grandpas. Put those chuckles here.

We all know a few "funnies" out of the mouths of grandmas and grandpas. Put those chuckles here.

# 5B

# Senior Humor-Fiction (Jokes)

An elderly couple stopped for gas on an out-of-state auto trip. After the filling station attendant asked the driver, "What can I do for you, sir?"

His hard of hearing wife said, "What did he say?"

Her husband explained. After filling the tank the attendant, while collecting payment, said, "I see by your license plate you're from Michigan. Whereabouts?"

When the attendant left, the driver's wife again asked, "What did he say?"

Her husband told her, adding, "I told him we're from Kalamazoo."

When the attendant returned with the man's change he chuckled, "I was in Kalamazoo about 40 years ago and dated a woman who must have been the worst kisser in the country."

As they pulled out onto the highway the lady again asked, "What did he say?"

Her husband replied, "He said he thinks he knows you."

෨ ෬ ෨ ෬

As we get older there are three things that begin to leave us. One is memory and ... er ... uh ... I forget the other two.

෨ ෬ ෨ ෬

The golfer at an executive country club didn't want the caddy assigned to him by the caddymaster. "He's too old and won't be able to see my drives. I hit a long ball and need a caddy with good eyesight."

The caddymaster assured the golfer the caddy had good eyesight, saying, "Trust me. Use him."

On the first tee the golfer nailed one, but never saw where the ball went. He asked caddy, "Did you see it?"

The caddy answered, "I certainly did."

Golfer: "Where'd it go?" caddy: "I forget."

෩ ෬ ෩ ෬

A retired couple was driving to Florida in their van, the driver's wife sitting in the extreme rear. A state policeman, sirens blaring and lights blinking, pulled the van over. He excitedly told the driver, "Sir, your wife fell out of the rear door ten miles back on the highway."

The retiree sighed, "Thank god, I thought I had gone deaf."

There are a multitude of jokes about the elderly. Write your favorite one, or two, here.

# 6
# Wit At Work

In the overseas operations of General Motors a sales manager was surveying his staff to learn who might be interested in an overseas assignment. When George, a sales engineer who had migrated to the United States from Scotland, was asked if he was willing to go overseas he replied, "I am overseas."

Our entire department was gathered around a co-worker as the company's president was presenting him with his 25 Year watch. After the presentation the recipient was asked to say a few words. He did, ending with, "I still remember my first day. After dressing to come to work I was standing at the kitchen sink, my mother combing my hair … "

ഇ ര ഇ ര

My co-worker, Bob Pratt disclosed that another man in our office had changed his name many years ago. After he told me this man's former name I said, with a hushed tone to my voice, "Well, I changed my name years ago too." As he leaned toward me, I confided, "It used to be Pratt."

ഇ ര ഇ ര

My daughter was working temporarily for her husband as a receptionist at his office. While she was talking to someone on the telephone her husband told her he was leaving to take a few clients to lunch. Linda said, "Okay, but I may not be here when you return. I'm leaving at 2:30."

As she returned to her telephone conversation the man she was talking to asked, "How do you get a job like that, leaving at 2:30?"

Linda replied, "I sleep with the boss."

                        ಸಿ ಛ ಸಿ ಛ

In a merger of their overseas operations General Motors relocated 200 employees from New York to Detroit. One of the Michiganian secretaries was named Denise. She soon grew tired of hearing New Yorkers asking her, "Hey Denise, where's da nephew?"

                        ಸಿ ಛ ಸಿ ಛ

"I'm sorry; he's not in his office. May I have him call you?" said the secretary of the man I was calling. After giving her my name and phone number she asked me to spell my name. I kiddingly responded, "That's B-i-c-k-6-m-e-y-e-r." Without questioning my spelling she said, "I'll have him call you, sir."

                        ಸಿ ಛ ಸಿ ಛ

My nephew was on the job as a salesman in a large hardware store when a customer who happened to be an old friend approached.

After asking one another about their wives and bringing each up to date on their wives, they got down to business. The customer needed some parts for his humidifier as well as some tips on installing them. As they walked together toward the cashier my nephew said, "You have to take good care of them or they're a pain in the neck."

His friend asked, "Humidifiers or wives?"

෩ ෬ ෩ ෬

At the time of the aforementioned transfer from New York to Detroit the employees interested in relocating were entitled to one or more long weekends in the Detroit area to seek living accommodations. One single woman who had taken such a trip was surrounded by fellow workers on her return to the office. She announced to all, "I'm not relocating. I wouldn't live in Michigan. It's too flat."

Knowing she lives in Manhattan, one co-worker said, "That's true. It doesn't have all the snow-capped mountains you're used to seeing in Manhattan."

෩ ෬ ෩ ෬

About one dozen people were impatiently and silently waiting for the down elevator in our Manhattan office building at 5 P.M. One employee asked our boss, standing next to him, "Would you believe I bought this coat in Switzerland 22 years ago?"

The boss, head tilted for a better look at the coat, replied, "Yes, I believe it."

ஓ ෬ ஓ ෬

Many years ago a fellow employee had a second job selling peanuts at Yankee Stadium during the baseball season on weekends and at night games. Given the opportunity to work a World Series game on a weekday afternoon he called the office the morning of the game to tell my boss he was sick and would not be able to work that day.

As he carried peanuts up and down the aisles of Yankee Stadium a familiar voice called, "Hey peanuts." He turned to make the sale – it was his boss.

ஓ ෬ ஓ ෬

My supervisor returned from the bank after making a withdrawal, asking me how to spell "forty." After spelling it for her she blushingly confided, "Well, I wanted to take out forty dollars, but I didn't know if it was spelled f-o-r-t-y or f-o-u-r-t-y, so I withdrew fifty."

೸ ೧೩ ೸ ೧೩

It was Valentine's Day at the office. I told a co-worker that I was to spend the evening at the home of my fiancé's parents where it was a family tradition to gather and distribute homemade Valentines to one another. The following day my friend at the office asked, "Well, did you have a good time last night at little-house-on-the-prairie?"

೸ ೧೩ ೸ ೧೩

One of my wife's job functions was to gather machine assembly prints from each department. When prints were not received when due she had to telephone the respective department. On those occasions when the prints were still not ready she would sing frustratingly to her contact person, "Some day my prints will come."

A group of us regularly lunched together. One day I told them what I had done right after my wife went to bed. I walked into our bedroom with a glass of water and an aspirin, offering them to Phyllis.

Phyllis: What's that for?
Me: Your headache.
Phyllis: I don't have a headache.
Me: Aha, I gotcha.

Laughing, one of my friends was determined to pull it on his wife. Ralph gave us a daily report, frustratingly explaining that he always grew tired and went to bed before his wife, Terry. Finally, one day he told us, "Guess what? Last night Terry went up to bed before I did so I quickly grabbed the aspirin and water. As I was about to take them upstairs she called down to me, 'Ralph, are you coming up?' when I answered, 'Yes,' she said, 'Bring me an aspirin and some water.'"

When I entered our normally busy local bakery I was pleased to see I was the only customer. As I pointed to a tray of cookies and began to order some I was stopped by the young, well trained girl behind the counter. "I'm sorry, you have to take a number first."

Looking around the store again I explained, "But I'm the only customer here."

She repeated, "You must take a number."

Somewhat perplexed, I took the next plastic tag, bearing No. 9. As she flipped over No. 9 on the wall she announced, "Nine is next, may I help you?"

༄ ༅ ༄ ༅

Our town's road crew is very efficient. One summer as I took my daily bicycle ride I often rode past the remains of a very large turtle. It lay there for many weeks, its shell crushed and flattened by many cars. One day there was a new white line running along the edge of the pavement, painted right over the turtle.

༄ ༅ ༄ ༅

Back in the 1950s, if you dialed WE6-1212, you would hear a recording that provided the current temperature and a weather forecast. Many people did not know you could reach the recording simply by dialing WE6 followed by any four digits, not necessarily 1212. My friend and co-worker, Harry, apparently was one of the "unknowing." As I stood at his desk one day a pretty secretary strolled by. Harry whispered to me, "I'd like to plant a big kiss on her."

Kiddingly, I said, "I'm going to call Arlene (his fiancée) and tell her what you said."

Harry sneered, "Go ahead and call her. Her work number is 123-4567." Reaching for his phone I called his bluff by quickly dialing WE6 instead of 123, then asked Harry, "What are the last four numbers?" He repeated them and I slowly dialed 4567 as he watched. When the weather recording came on I pretended to be talking to Arlene's supervisor and asked to speak to Arlene "Jones." Waiting about ten seconds I repeated Harry's comment about the pretty secretary to Arlene – or so he thought. Saying, "Yes, he's right here," I handed the phone to Harry.

The frightened look on his face was replaced with relief when he heard the weather recording.

ೞ ೧೩ ೞ ೧೩

Jim, a young Marine veteran from World War II, began his career in the Billing Department of General Motors. One of his functions as a billing clerk was to sort a stack of car invoices, six copies for each car clipped together. One copy of each was set aside for the Credit Department, two copies for Accounting, two for the automobile dealer and one for the Billing file. After "breaking down" invoices every day for many months Jim bet a co-worker he could do this part of his job blindfolded. As he did, our billing manager, returning from a late lunch, strolled through the office. Seeing blindfolded Jim determinedly zipping invoices into those four stacks and knowing Jim's reputation for being skilled and fast with a sense of humor, the manager just shook his head and grinned. A few weeks later another clerk who performed the same job, handling dealers in a different zone, went to the manager seeking a pay increase.

His prepared presentation to the boss, "I have a college degree and do my job without error," was countered with, "You want a raise? Why, I have a man who can do that job blindfolded."

೩೦ ೦೩ ೩೦ ೦೩

After a successful business year a vice president invited many of us to a celebratory cocktail party. He arranged for one man to circulate among all in attendance, taking pictures of small groups standing around the large room. The imaginative sense of humor of Jim came into play as he slipped into each group with a wide grin. Eventually, the photographer caught on and politely asked him to step aside, waiting until he did before snapping the picture. As the man with the camera continued to move about the room Jim followed discreetly (sneakily?) behind him. As he lifted the camera to his eye Jim would briskly step into the group or, crouching behind them, stand up behind and between two men a moment before the photo was snapped. When the pictures were circulated around the office a few days later imagine the uproar when, knowing Jim's humor, everyone saw his smiling face in almost every picture. ಸಿ ಆ ಸಿ ಆ

It was in the 1960s. My secretary's husband was a plain-clothes policeman, ambitious and anxious to nab a thief. He parked his convertible in a high crime neighborhood with some attractive packages on the front seat. He then staked out his own car from around a nearby corner. It wasn't long before the stack of packages caught a pedestrian's eye. Looking around and seeing no one the pedestrian quickly pulled out a knife and slashed the convertible top to gain entry. The frustrated policeman ran to his car screaming, "You dumb crook. Why didn't you try the door? It isn't locked."

ಸಿ ಆ ಸಿ ಆ

There were eight of us at the meeting, back in the days when smoking was permitted in the office. Some one remarked that no one was smoking.

All eight admitted they were former smokers, each relating the difficulties he had fighting his addiction to tobacco. One man bragged, "Giving up smoking was easy for me. In fact, I did it three times."

The pressures of work are often relieved with pranks. Which are your favorites?

# 7

# Political Humor

After many years of driving I had not learned to stay within the speed limit. The car with the flashing lights pulled me over. A policeman politely asked for my driver's license and registration. After checking these documents she returned them to me with only a warning, adding, "I read your letters to editor in the newspaper." Obviously (and luckily) the policeman was a Republican. If a Democrat I would have been "nailed."

*"Something that I was not aware that happened suddenly turned out not to have happened."*

– British Prime Minister John Major

*"There are more crimes in Britain now, due to the huge rise in the crime rate."*

– British Labor Party leader Neil Kinnock

*"We all know a leopard can't change his stripes."*

– Vice President/ Presidential candidate Al Gore

JOKES:

In one of his campaign tours during the primary season a Presidential candidate spoke to a large group at a Native American Indian reservation. While speaking there were many cries of "Mooda, mooda." At the conclusion of his speech one of the leaders took the politician on a tour of the reservation.

As they approached the bullpen the leader cautioned him, "Please be careful. Don't step in the mooda."

ਸ਼੦ ੦੩ ਸ਼੦ ੦੩

Upon entering heaven a leading politician's wife noticed an abundance of clocks. She asked an angel, "Why so many clocks?"

The angel explained, "There is a clock for every one on Earth. Each time a person lies, his or her clock advances one minute. When they die their clock stops and we can easily count the lies told in their lifetime. That clock, for example, was Abraham Lincoln's. It reads two minutes past twelve, indicating he told only two lies in his lifetime. This clock was Mother Theresa's. Both hands are still on twelve because she never told a lie."

Said the politician's wife, "That is very interesting. May I see my husband's clock?"

The angel replied, "No, I am sorry, but Jesus keeps your husband's clock in his bedroom to use as a ceiling fan."

ਸ਼੦ ੦੩ ਸ਼੦ ੦੩

Three clergymen of different faiths were debating the issue of when life begins. The first stated, "Life begins at the moment of conception."

"I must disagree, said the second, "Life begins at birth."

The third clergyman corrected them. "You're both wrong. Life begins when all the children have left home and the dog dies."

ಸಿ ಅ ಸಿ ಅ

The short politician, at five feet six inches, boasted, "I'm six feet tall." Seeing everyone raises one eyebrow, he added, "I'm just short for my height."

Politicians are often funny, sometimes unintentionally. Have you heard any of their gaffes? Jot them down. Oh, and be sure to be politically correct

# 8

# Sidesplitting Sports Stuff

Marilyn Monroe was in Yankee Stadium rooting for the Detroit Tigers in a three game series in August 2006. The Tigers left fielder, Craig Monroe, had flown his mother to New York to see the big city and to see her son play against the Yankees. The name of Monroe's mother is Marilyn.

On a nice spring day we often took a walk in Central Park at lunchtime, near our offices in Manhattan, and watched a few innings of a softball game in the Broadway Show League. Phil Rizzuto, the former great Yankee shortstop and the current play-by-play announcer for them, played shortstop for the CBS team. A batter hit a ground ball to Rizzuto with a man on first base. He fielded it flawlessly and made a perfect toss to the second baseman for a forceout, but the second baseman dropped the ball. I called out "E-6," the scoring symbol for an error by the shortstop. I guess an error in the Show League is as embarrassing as an error in the Major Leagues because Rizzuto looked at me and called back, "Oh no."

I have a reputation for throwing my golf club after a poorly hit ball. Very immature of me. One time, after hitting a ground ball down the fairway, I stood there frustrated, but club still in hand.

The other half of my foursome was parked in their golf cart behind me, watching. The driver called, "Hey Bob, you want to throw your club in front of me so I can run over it?"

I answered, "I have a better idea" and proceeded to lay on my back in front of his cart, saying, "Run me over."

༶ ༶ ༶ ༶

Lucy Lawless was singing "The Star Spangled Banner" at a Detroit Red Wings- Anaheim Mighty Ducks hockey playoff game, televised locally on Channel 50. Lawless was almost finished when her top popped out of her tight-fitting, flag-draped costume. Producers were stunned as Lawless' breast waved in the air while she concluded with "… the home of the brave." Channel 50 received 11 phone calls from viewers, one complaint and ten requests for a rebroadcast.

༶ ༶ ༶ ༶

Three thousand feet above the ground, I was about to make my first parachute jump – at age 60. Terrified, I listened to the instructor, "As you place your feet on the step outside the door, grab the wing strut.

Then hang from the strut with both hands and look at me. When I nod, let go."

My fear heightening, I asked, "What happens if I fall during this maneuver?"

He smiled, "You're dressed for it."

ಐ ಔ ಐ ಔ

It was during a game in a senior citizen softball league. One of our opponents looked and walked like he was about 88 years old. As he stepped to the plate I said to my nearest teammate, "I hope he gets a hit."

When my teammate asked, "Why?"

I replied, "Because his parents are at the game."

ಐ ಔ ಐ ಔ

It was about 45 years ago when the New York football Giants had a big fullback named Ed Modzelewski. His nickname, given to him at the southern college he attended, was Big Mo. When his brother arrived at the same college he was called Little Mo. The third and last brother arrived at that college and, of course, was called No Mo.

The ball of my golfing opponent had rolled to rest against the 150 yard marker, a 4" x 4" white stake planted alongside the fairway. As he set up in his stance, preparing to hit the ball, I decided to be charitable and allow him to move the ball away from the stake. I said, "Go ahead and move it." My large opponent happily grabbed the stake in a bear hug and tore it from the ground.

At a swim meet in Minnesota between two colleges a swimmer dove into the pool after forgetting to tie the strings in his swimsuit. As it slipped down his legs he kicked it off. He continued to swim and won the race, but was disqualified for a uniform violation. He later explained, "I kept swimming because we were doing the butterfly. I would have stopped if it was the backstroke."

When she was a member of the Troy Community Chorus my wife attended weekly rehearsals. Recently a teammate on my senior softball team called to advise me he wouldn't be able to make practice.

When he asked to speak to me my wife told him, "He's already left for rehearsal."

※ ☙ ※ ☙

One of the men in my retiree golfing group scores consistently in the 80s while I am content when I shoot under 100. One day I asked him, "Jack, what is the biggest flaw I have?" without any hesitation he said, "Well, it's when you get out of your car in the parking lot."

※ ☙ ※ ☙

Our softball team plays two game each week. The wife of one of my teammates comes to every game. I once asked her why she comes to every game. Before she could answer another team member interjected, "So she doesn't have to kiss him goodbye."

※ ☙ ※ ☙

Embarrassing moments: It was the championship game of the teen league in our town's football program. As one of the game's officials I was umpire, stationed in the defensive backfield. The running back took a handoff from his quarterback and plowed through the line.

Gang-tackled by three players, he fell in front of me. I blew my whistle, ending the play ... but I never saw a defensive player strip the ball from him, who was now streaking in the opposite direction for a certain touchdown ... except for the fact I had blown the whistle ending the play.

ಸಿ ಬಿ ಸಿ ಬಿ

In golf, on par three holes, it was necessary to wave the next foursome to hit their tee shots after our foursome's balls were on the green. First, we picked up our balls, marking their spot on the green with a coin or a ball marker. After the four hit their tee shots we walked back onto the green, golf balls in hand, to place them where they had been. Embarrassed, I could not find my marker, a dime. I called, "Anyone see a dime?" without a moment's hesitation one of them said," There are two nickels over here."

ಸಿ ಬಿ ಸಿ ಬಿ

When picking up my new set of golf clubs, made especially for me, I asked, "How many strokes will they take off my game?"

The salesman replied, "Well, with practice, up to ten strokes."

I said, "Heck, I could have practiced with my old set."

℘ ℭ ℘ ℭ

Bob Houlihan, a humble golfing friend enjoyed telling this one about himself. In a large corporate golf outing the famous pro, Chi Chi Rodriguez, was persuaded to play one hole with each foursome. "When he played with us," Bob related, "his ball and mine were both about 150 yards from the green. I was away and, swinging first, put the ball on the green. Chi Chi said, 'Nice shot.' He then hit his ball onto the green and I said, 'Nice shot.' But I used a 3-wood and Chi Chi used an 8-iron."

℘ ℭ ℘ ℭ

A friend and co-worker, who had a great sense of humor, had been on a day's fishing excursion off Long Island on the Atlantic Ocean. Back at the office Monday morning, I asked him how his day at sea was. Bill replied, "Great, even though I caught nothing."

After plenty of enjoyable food and drink I relaxed by laying on a shelf at the stern of the boat. Suddenly, a large swell in the waves tipped the boat causing me to roll off into the sea. There were sharks all around me ... but ... fortunately, I happened to have a knife in my mouth."

೫ ෬ ೫ ෬

## JOKES:

A man and his wife were playing golf when he sliced his drive behind a barn that was between his ball and the green. As he prepared to chip his ball safely back onto the fairway his wife suggested, "Here's a challenge. I'll open the doors at each end of the barn and you can go for the green, through the barn." She did that and took a safe position inside the barn, however, his well hit ball struck a beam in the barn, ricocheting and striking his wife in the head, killing her. Coincidentally, about one year later he was golfing with a new friend when he sliced another drive behind the same barn. When the friend suggested he drive the ball through the barn the widower said, "Oh no, not after what happened the last time I tried that. I took a nine on the hole."

Knowing her time on Earth was short the sick wife asked her husband, "When I die, will you remarry?"

The husband replied, "In all honesty, I may."

Wife: "Would you share this house with your next wife?"

Husband: "You know how practical I am. That would be the practical thing to do."

Wife: "Would you give her my fur coat?"

Husband: "If it fit her, I guess so."

Wife: "Would you allow her to use my golf clubs?"

Husband: "Oh no, she's lefthanded."

Jesus and Moses were playing a round of golf. After teeing up his ball on a par three hole, Jesus reached for his eight iron. Moses cautioned Him, "Sir, you'll never clear the pond in front of the green with that club."

Jesus replied," Yes I will. I saw Tiger Woods use an eight iron at this hole on TV."

He swung and connected, but the ball splashed into the pond. Moses parted the water and retrieved the ball. Jesus teed up the ball and again prepared to hit it with the eight iron.

Again Moses cautioned Him not to use an eight iron. Again, Jesus reminded Moses that Tiger Woods cleared this pond with an eight iron. Again, "Splash." Jesus told Moses, about to part the water," Never mind. I'll get it myself." He walked onto the water to get His ball. As he did this, another foursome approached the tee.

One of them asked Moses, "Who does that guy think he is, Jesus?"

Moses said, "No, He thinks He's Tiger Woods."

೮೦ ೦ಽ ೮೦ ೦ಽ

Throughout a Little League baseball game one mother mercilessly shrieked her disagreement with the umpire's decisions on all close calls that went against her son's team. Her team ultimately lost the game. As the sweaty umpire, a volunteer father, walked off the field she called after him, "If you were my husband I'd give you poison."

The umpire turned toward her, saying, "Lady, if I was your husband I'd take it."

Humorous incidents in sports may be related here. If you haven't been active in sports, turn to the next page.

# 9
# Vacation Heehaws

While vacationing in the Pocono Mountains in Pennsylvania we came upon a gift shop with a sign in front, reading:

"Penny candy – $1.39 ½ pound."

࿇ ࿇ ࿇ ࿇

Just a few minutes after leaving home for a summer motor trip my wife, who always sleeps with two pillows, blurted, "I forgot to bring an extra pillow." Obligingly, I made a U-turn and, eventually, we had made our second departure from home. Only minutes later Sweetie-pie sheepishly uttered, "I don't have my pills." Another U-turn followed by a third departure.

That evening while relaxing at poolside and chatting with a fellow traveler, we were comparing our day's motoring. In reply to his question, "What time did you leave home?"

I straight-faced "At 9:00, 9:10 and 9:20."

࿇ ࿇ ࿇ ࿇

During an auto tour of New England our family stopped for lunch in a small town. In as much as the restaurant had no appropriate seat for our three-year-old son I asked the waitress to bring a telephone book for him to sit on, a common alternative for a booster seat back home in New York City. She soon returned, a perplexed look on her face, and handed me the local phone book, about one eighth of an inch thick.

ಙ ಛ ಙ ಛ

While driving through Indiana we stopped for gas in a small town. A large sign on the front window of the filling station, easily read from the gas pumps, bore a list of eight names. Above the names were the words, "THE NAMES OF THOSE WHO HAVE WRITTEN BAD CHECKS ARE:"

ಙ ಛ ಙ ಛ

My propensity to speed while driving was, again, not harnessed. We were zipping along on Interstate 75, en route to Florida from Michigan, when we reached a monstrous traffic jam in Tennessee. After a half-hour of creeping and crawling we finally arrived at the cause of the "jam" – a bad accident. Two severely damaged cars, a wrecker and four or five police cars were blocking I75 except for one lane. After we merged with traffic and passed the accident scene the highway in front of us was wide open. I pressed the accelerator to the floor, trying to make up some of the lost time. Phyllis cautioned me, "You're gonna get a ticket."

All knowingly, I replied, "Not a chance. All the cops are back there at the accident." At that very moment my rear view mirror showed a car bearing down on me with flashing lights. The Tennessee State police, knowing how we drivers think, nailed me.

ঞ ৎ ঞ ৎ

Think about it. Something funny must have happened while on vacation when everyone is relaxed.

# 10
# One-Liners

You're only young once, but you can be immature forever.

    ಬಲಬಲ

Sign in a closed-down bookstore: "Words failed us."

    ಬಲಬಲ

Laugh and the world laughs with you, snore and you sleep alone.

    ಬಲಬಲ

Sign in a Royal Oak, Michigan restaurant:
"Courteous and efficient self-service"

A Detroit television channel interrupted a show with a news brief: "In Pontiac, police shot a man with a knife."

Over the door of our local bakery is the sign "TROY BAKERY underneath of which is the lettering "Get your buns in here."

My favorite word is "free." My second favorite word is "discount."

As I tuned into a Detroit radio station for the weather report I heard, "Today's high will be between 56 and 60. The current reading is 62."

When your shoes and socks come off, your toes sorta say "Thanks."

I just sat there with my teeth in my mouth.

ଛ ଓଃ ଛ ଓଃ

I read somewhere, "Behind every great man is a woman rolling her eyes." Not so! My wife rolls her eyes often and it hasn't helped me at all.

ଛ ଓଃ ଛ ଓଃ

The harder you work, the luckier you get.

ଛ ଓଃ ଛ ଓଃ

There is a close correlation between getting up in the morning and getting up in the world.

# 11A

# Military Humor – Fiction

After donning his suit of armor to go to battle a knight put a chastity belt on his wife. He gave the key to the belt to his trusted friend, telling him, "If I should not return give this key to my wife." The knight was only mile or two out of town when a cloud of dust appeared behind him. The lone rider was the trusted friend who called to the knight, "You gave me the wrong key."

What is your favorite one-liner? Pass it on here.

As a U.S. Navy destroyer chugged into a French port a tug boat waited to guide it to be docked. At the appropriate time the destroyer's captain used a bullhorn to ask that the tug boat be brought alongside the ship. When the tug failed to respond he realized the captain of the small boat did not understand, English. Using the destroyer's internal communication system, he asked that anyone aboard the ship who spoke French report to the bridge immediately.

In minutes a seaman appeared and, with a salute, said, "I speak French, Sir."

Handing him the bullhorn, the captain ordered the seaman, "Tell him to bring the tug boat alongside the ship."

In a clear, amplified voice, the seaman said, "Breeng ze tug boat alonzide ze sheep."

# Know any military jokes?

# 11B

# Military Humor – True Tales And "The Sarge"

It was my first day in the army during the Korean War, part of a group of disheveled draftees. A corporal was taking roll call. When he called "SanAntonio" the new recruit answered "Here."

Hesitating with his roll call the corporal, with a smirk, asked, "Do you have any relatives in Texas?"

Private SanAntonio strightfaced, "It's possible. We're like horse manure, we're all over the place."

℘ ℘ ℘ ℘

A group of us were discussing equal rights. A lady feminist, obviously misunderstanding one man's leanings on the subject, scolded him good-naturedly for being a male chauvinist. "Me?" he grinned, "I, who often brags about my niece, a cop on the local police force, and my nephew, a nurse in the army?"

℘ ℘ ℘ ℘

Drafted during the Korean War, Bill (not his real name) and I became army buddies when we wound up in the machine gun platoon of "M" Company, 155th Regiment in the 31st Infantry Division. We both disliked the hard work, the tedious repetitive training and the discipline, but were determined to be good soldiers. We "bitched" as did every one of our fellow soldiers.

After basic training at Ft. Jackson, S.C. our skills and physical shape were further sharpened with specialized training.

We were then made combat-ready with month long maneuvers at Ft. Bragg, N.C. It was during these maneuvers that I lost respect for Bill. Believing that he was getting too close to boarding a troop ship to Korea, he concocted a plan to receive a medical discharge. He was going to "go bananas," as he put it. One night we were bedded down, side by side, on a mattress of gathered pine needles. We were surrounded by our platoon. And the company commander was in the area. Bill announced to me in a whisper, "The time is ripe, Bob, here I go" and he emitted a blood curdling scream. He jumped to his feet and grabbed his head as if in agony. The scene was chaotic as our C.O., a captain, our platoon leader, a lieutenant, and squad leader, a sergeant hustled him off to the medics. "His choice," I thought to myself as, exhausted from the day, I slept soundly through the night.

After our C-ration breakfast the platoon was preparing to again do battle with the "aggressors," GIs trained to emulate the enemy, when Bill was returned to the platoon. Surprised, I asked, "What happened?"

He sullenly replied, "They insisted my symptoms were a reaction to all the dust I breathed in during our forced march yesterday, so ... here I am."

৩০ ෬ ৩০ ෬

The perseverance and self-discipline of Larry Page is a fascinating story. Page, while attempting to help a fellow soldier in Vietnam was injured by a land mine. In a coma for nine days, in a military hospital for 14 months, blind, paralyzed and partially deaf – he came back to clean sewers by hand and worked himself up to the Director of the Huntington Woods, Michigan Department of Public Works. What a guy, a man to be admired by his fellow Americans.

## "The Sarge"

Jim Shearin and I were working buddies for General Motors Overseas Operations in New York for 31 years. It was early one morning, my first week on the job in July 1947, when Jim approached my desk, saying, "Hey fella, you want to see something? Follow me." He led me to an outer staircase and pointed out of the window.

Across a large courtyard in the window of an apartment building was a woman doing her morning exercises, wearing nothing. We enjoyed a hearty laugh together, the first of many laughs. It was my introduction to Jim, a man with a keen, imaginative sense of humor.

One day we were sitting at a table in a cafeteria, our trays of food in front of us. A well dressed lady put her tray on a nearby table, then left to get a glass of water. Jim's timing was perfect. As she returned she found Jim sitting in front of her tray, knife and fork poised as if he was about to enjoy her food.

As she screamed, "Mister, that's my food."

Jim went into his act, standing and saying, "Gee, I'm sorry ma'am I thought it was mine." He returned to our table with a wide grin on his face as I had another hearty laugh from my buddy's sense of humor

During a business trip Jim and I were killing time in our hotel's cocktail lounge. A gorgeous young woman joined us. After chatting with us for about five minutes she asked Jim, "Why don't we go up to your room?"

Jim asked, "How much?"

When she said, "One hundred dollars" Jim grinned, "Okay, I can use the money."

He was a talented stand-up comic. At the annual company golf outings, bachelor parties or goodbye parties for those transferred overseas Jim usually made a speech chock full of anecdotes and one-liners that kept his co-workers in non-stop laughter.

I often called him "Sarge." A marine veteran of World War II, Jim loved the marines and chose to remain in the active reserves. Consequently, when I was drafted into the army during the Korean War Jim was activated and also served in Korea. We both returned to General Motors, but Jim was again activated during the Vietnam conflict. A veteran of three wars, he attained the rank of Master Sergeant, the highest rank below a commissioned officer.

The Sarge was known for his neatness and cleanliness – of self, clothing and car as well as an orderly desk and efficient work habits.

I don't know if this was the result of his upbringing or his military training, but he was always ready for inspection.

Sarge was always in top physical shape. No one in our large office staff could do more pushups than him and he was the only one who could do a one-hand pushup. He was the arm wrestling champ. At office parties, after a few drinks, someone would almost always challenge the champ, hoping to dethrone him. It never happened. Jim simply grinned after each victory and asked for another beer.

When GM transferred me to Detroit the Sarge elected early retirement. The years passed, but we kept in touch by telephone. He was devastated by the loss of his wife of many years. He became forgetful, telling me, "I can't even drive to the supermarket because I can't find my way home." It became necessary for the Sarge to live with his daughter, Holly, and to spend his days in a senior day care center.

The last time I called Jim, Holly answered the phone. Before calling him to the phone she prepared me." He definitely has Alzheimer's and may not remember you."

Thankfully, he remembered me and during our brief conversation again said, "I love you, Bob." He had said it once before, some years ago. Hearing that rugged Marine Sergeant tell me that he loved me remains one of the proudest moments of my life.

God bless you, Sarge, I love you.

Active duty in the military is not as common as it once was. If not applicable, turn the page. If you have a true story. Humorous or inspiring, this is the place for it.

# 12

# ... And That's The Way It Was!

It was my ritual, since I had first retired and weather permitting, to take a morning bicycle ride. My bike jaunts were a pleasure, more enjoyable than all the other aerobic type exercises I had indulged in.

This particular morn it was sheer joy as I cruised under the warm sun, not yet high in the sky. The cool, still air, provoked by my cruising speed, became a delightful breeze.

My perspiration from the exercise and the sun was lifted from me by the cool breeze. Conditions were perfect.

Ahead of me a man and his dog were strolling along, the man on the shoulder of the road as I was, his dog sniffing something on the road. A car was speeding towards them from the opposite direction. As it drew closer I began to realize the possibility of a tragedy. The pooch was entranced by whatever lay on the road. His owner, apparently engrossed in his thoughts, was oblivious to his pet's danger. I'll never know why the driver of the car failed to slow down.

I pedaled as quickly as I could toward the dog, my thumb leaning on my horn button. He looked up at me, stood transfixed momentarily, then darted towards his master as the auto, brakes screeching, passed over the subject of the dog's sniffing, a dead woodchuck. Meanwhile, I swerved after the darting dog, lost my balance and tumbled at the man's feet as the car resumed speed.

As I worked myself to my feet I saw an elderly and quite homely man with a very concerned expression, asking, "Are you all right?"

Once he received my assurances I was not injured, a wide semi-toothless grin took over and he poured out his gratitude, Benjamin is my constant companion. I have no family. My life would be completely empty without him." He handed me a newspaper to hold while he reached into his two coat pockets. I couldn't help noticing the date on the newspaper, November 3, but the year was 2104. I chuckled inwardly at the obvious typo. His hands held a pair of dark green shoes made of a supple skin. He handed them to me, saying, "Since words are not enough, I have but one way to show my appreciation to you for saving Benjamin. Wear these shoes for one day and they will please you in a way that you can't imagine. Promise me that you will." It was a simple request and, not wanting to hurt his feelings, I agreed. The kindly gent turned and he and Benjamin resumed their interrupted stroll. I wheeled around and headed for home, somewhat perplexed, the green shoes in my bicycle basket.

The next morning I started for my bike and, finding the shoes still in the basket, remembered my promise. As I slipped them on I found them to be the most comfortable shoes I had ever worn. "Heck," I thought, "I'll skip my ride today and, instead, take a long walk." About a quarter of a mile from home I reached a wooded area with a narrow, little used path cutting through it. "A new route," I thought, "not at all appealing for bike riding." I entered it.

There was a mist ahead, so peaceful looking that I hurried my pace to break into it. The mist engulfed me. My green shoes quivered, causing a tingling sensation in my feet. I cautiously slowed my pace until I came through the mist.

I found myself strolling through the woods of Virginia way back in the year 1743. How I knew this I don't know, but my awareness of where I was and my place in time came to me just before the tingling in my feet subsided. Eventually I ambled onto a large, undeveloped plantation. The only sound of any life or activity on this hot, still summer day was a repetitious thunk, thunk, thunking noise.

I followed the sound 'till I came upon a youth of about nine, with axe in hand, aiming blow after blow at the slim trunk of a young cherry tree. As I watched, the tree fell to the ground.

An older boy appeared, bellowing, "Samuel, that was father's favorite cherry tree. Why did you chop it down?"

Samuel, much shorter and leaner than his older brother, his shirt wet with perspiration, replied somewhat hoarsely, "I just _had_ to have a hat full of those tasty, juicy cherries. I couldn't reach them nor could I climb the tree, so I chopped the tree down, George." (They were obviously completely unaware of my presence, as if I was unseen.)

That evening, after supper as dessert was being served by Mary Ball Washington, her husband, Augustine, sat straight up in his chair at the head of the table and, with a stern look about the table at his five children, asked, "Who chopped down my prize cherry tree today?" Without a moment's hesitation 11 year old George blurted, "Father, I cannot tell a lie. It was I." "Interesting," I mused, "that the Father of our country, credited with being such an honest youth for almost two and a half centuries was really more than that.

He lied to take the blame and the subsequent punishment for his younger brother.

... And that's the way it was!

I continued my stroll as a cloud settled upon me. I smiled, wondering, "What next?" After only a few steps the cloud lifted. I knew, somehow, that I had been whisked forward in time to 1876. I was in Montana territory, in an Indian village in a valley alongside Little Bighorn River. Why, there must have been over 1,000 wigwams. A pow-wow of Sioux leaders was in progress in a grassy clearing at riverside. It being June 25th with a bright sun and no breeze, some Indians wore only a breechcloth while others wore not even that. Each of them was smoking a long feathered pipe, but as I listened to their plans I knew they were not peace pipes. A stockily built Indian with a gnarled, rusted face was talking. It was obvious that he was "Chairman of the Board" as he easily commanded the attention of all present.

Although all chiefs wore the customary long feathered headdress, the "Chairman" wore a sole eagle feather. He spoke. "This brave ...," looking at a warrior squatting to his right, "...dared to penetrate the camp of about 250 white warriors while the moon was in the sky." (Although he spoke in the Sioux tongue, somehow I understood.) "They were having a tribal council such as we are now having. Their leader, called Colonel Custer by his men, told them he was sending an advance scout, at sunrise, to locate our village. He intends to surprise us, kill most of our braves and bring our tribe into reservations. He boasted of the glory that would be bestowed upon himself and his entire regiment."

The angry scowl on his face melted and became a smile as he continued. "Cunning Wolf, here, stole out of the camp and awaited Custer's scout, whom he slayed. Now <u>we</u> will surprise <u>them</u>, contrary to this Custer's plans. We will ambush them and I, sitting Bull, command you and your braves to kill every white trooper."

... And that's the way it was!

The fog again enveloped me and then dissolved in the cool air. It was Dayton, Ohio, just before the turn of the century. I was drawn into a bicycle shop operated by two brothers. The elder of the two, Wilbur, was talking. "Orville, where in tarnation did you come up with the zany idea that we can build a man-carrying machine to fly with built-in power?"

Orville, four years younger, replied with some embarrassment, "Well ... in the Katzenjammer Kids funnies the two kids built a power-driven glider that flew from one to the other. I figured ... it's reasonable that such a machine could be built, but on a larger scale to carry the weight of a man."

"Yup, I saw that comic," said Wilbur, "and I chuckled at the idea. Heck, comics are for fun and laughs. Don't take 'em seriously. Next thing you know, there'll be a comic strip with flying ships darting into space, maybe even landing up there on the moon. I'll snicker at that comic too, 'cause you know it can never happen."

"Of course not," laughed Orville, "but let's take up gilding and, who knows, if we're successful at gliding we'll think about the Katzenjammer Kids' idea."

... And that's the way it was!

I was again "misted" to another place. The feeling that I saw somehow "home" was confirmed by that mysterious inner knowledge of my place and year in time. It was the village of Detroit, Territory of Michigan, in the year 1815. It was a delightful evening, the sun retiring in the western sky, a few clouds nestled just to the right of the sun, a lone kite reaching towards them.

Traffic was heavy, but had a calming effect on me. I sat on a bench in a park at roadside and watched a steady current of carriages flow by, the only sound the cadence of horse's hooves clippity-clopping on the dirt road. As enjoyable and relaxing as this scene was, curiosity lifted me to my feet.

The park at my back, many interesting buildings were across the street. I darted across, nimbly side-stepping an oncoming carriage. The driver cursed me as he passed.

"What?" I realized, "I'm no longer unseen as I was in my previous experiences." Luckily, because of the assortment of nationalities and garb – American, British, French, Indian – I blended in somewhat in my casual 2004 attire.

I peered into the dirty window of a tavern where many men were relaxing after their workday; talking, smoking, drinking, playing cards or bowling on the green behind the tavern.

Continuing along the footpath I passed the closed shops of a tailor, shoemaker, wigmaker and a general store. I came to a church, apparently doubling as the village meeting hall. The townspeople were beginning to assemble inside, coming from every direction by carriage, horse and on foot. I entered. Trying to be as inconspicuous as possible, I took a seat in the rear and waited.

Soon, the chairman began the meeting. The subject was the conversion of the village of Detroit to an incorporated city. A motion to incorporate was seconded and, after a brief discussion, was almost unanimously carried. A motion was then made, and seconded, to retain the name "Detroit" for the new city.

Unexpectedly, there was a lengthy discussion opposing this name. Many of the townspeople preferred that the new city be called "Pontchartrain." Listening, I learned that the village of Detroit had previously been Fort Detroit. Before that it had been established by the French explorer Cadillac as Fort Pontchartrain. Their arguments were convincing as, when the "Detroit" motion was finally put to a vote, there were an equal number of hands "against" as there were "for."

    A heated discussion followed, but I barely listened. My mind had drifted back to 2004 where I envisioned the Pontchartrain Tigers, the Pontchartrain Lions, the Pontchartrain Pistons and the Pontchartrain Red Wings. "No, it couldn't happen!" I thought. "Detroit" had to win. Finally, the speaker put the matter to "one final vote" as he put it. "All those in favor of Pontchartrain?" A count of hands showed no change, a like number as before. The speaker, shaking his head in frustration, proclaimed, "If the vote is again a tie this will be tabled until next week … All those in favor of Detroit?"

As the count began I timidly lifted my hand. He completed his count of hands by loudly declaring, "It's Detroit! By one vote. The meeting is adjourned."

… And that's the way it was!

My experiences had exhausted me and, whether it was coincidence or because I had wished it, when the next mist that enveloped me had lifted, I was back in 2004 on the path in the wooded area near home, a northern suburb of Detroit. Night had fallen and I trudged home through the darkness. Home, I was too fatigued to do anything but peel off my clothing and collapse into bed.

I awoke the next morning famished, hurried through breakfast and slipped on my moccasin-like enchanted shoes. Impatience and curiosity tore at me. I couldn't wait to spend another day in my new shoes, wondering what pieces of history awaited me. As I walked out of my home awaiting me were Benjamin and his smiling master. The gent reminded me, "If you will remember, sir, I had asked you to wear those shoes for one day. Now that you have, I'm afraid that I must return with them,"

Very reluctantly, I slipped them off and hesitantly handed the shoes to him. He thrust them into his coat pockets. As he pulled his hands back out he carelessly tore the top edge off a newspaper that was folded and stashed inside one pocket. It floated to the ground. Without another word, he turned and walked away, Benjamin tagging along. As I watched, a cloud settled upon them. Almost immediately it lifted, but they were gone.

I picked up all that was left of them, the torn newspaper. It was one day later, November 4th, but the year was again 2104!

## The End

If you have always had a yen to try writing a short fantasy try it here. Once you try you may stretch your imagination beyond even what you may have expected. If so, grab a few sheets of paper to bring your fantasy to a proper conclusion. And thanks for reading this book to the very end.

The author rests after completing this book – with his Jack Russell Terrier who bites trucks